Let's Make Music

By Margaret Clyne and Rachel Griffiths

CELEBRATION PRESS
Pearson Learning Group

Contents

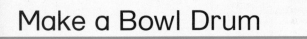

Introduction

Different musical instruments make different sounds.
Find out more by making some.

Make Bottle Shakers

You can make bottle shakers
that make musical sounds.

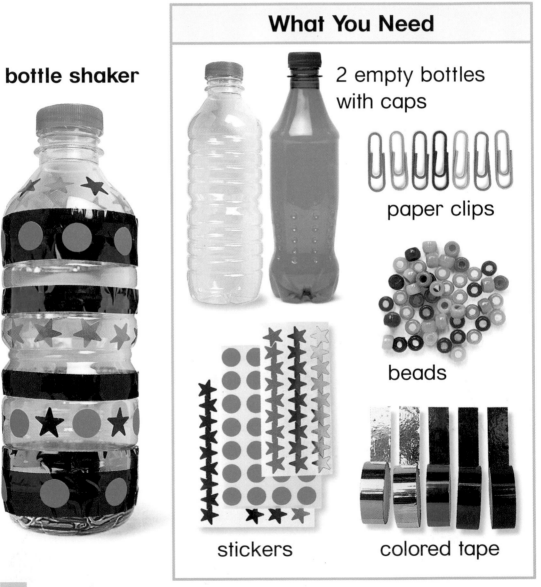

bottle shaker

What You Need

2 empty bottles
with caps

paper clips

beads

stickers

colored tape

1. Put a few paper clips in one bottle.

2. Put some beads in the second bottle.

3. Put the caps on the bottles.

4 Decorate the bottles with colored tape and stickers.

5 Shake your bottle shakers.

Compare the sounds of the shakers.
Are the sounds loud or quiet?

Make a Bowl Drum

You can make a drum to make musical sounds.

bowl drum

What You Need

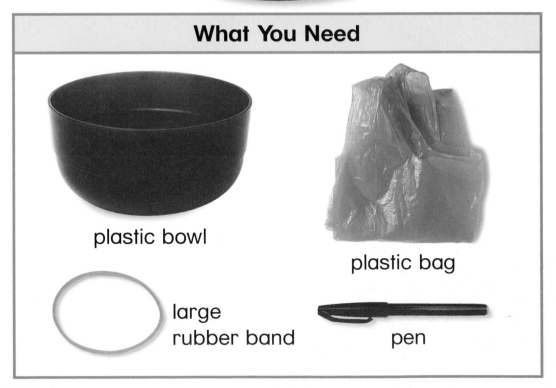

plastic bowl

plastic bag

large
rubber band

pen

① Fit the plastic bag over the bowl.

② Put the rubber band around it.

③ Pull the plastic bag tight.

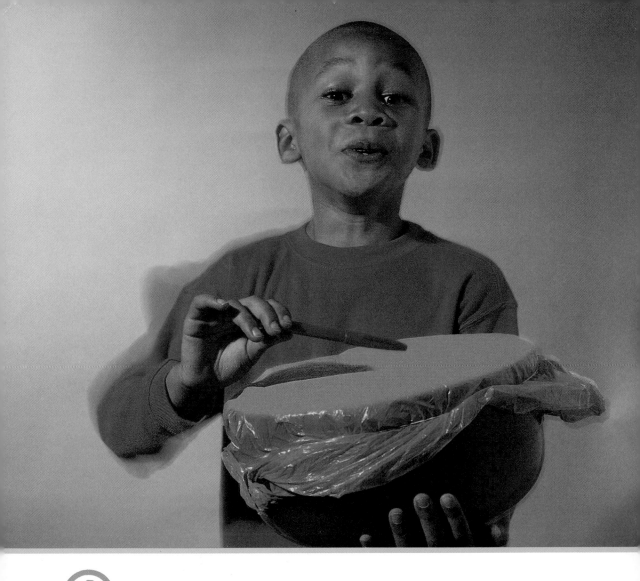

4) Hold the drum in one hand.

5) Tap the drum with the pen.

Listen to the sound the drum makes.

⑥ Pull the plastic bag tighter.

⑦ Tap the drum again.

Compare the sounds the drum makes.
Is one higher or lower than the other?

Make Bottle Pipes

You can make bottle pipes to make musical sounds.

bottle pipes

What You Need

6 glass bottles with narrow necks

cup

funnel

food coloring

① Line up the bottles.

② Pour water into the bottles
using the funnel.
Put a lot of water into some bottles.
Put a little water into some bottles.

 Add food coloring to the water in each bottle.

④ Blow air softly across the tops
of the bottle pipes.

5 Blow air over bottles with less water.

6 Blow air over bottles with more water.

Compare the sounds of the bottle pipes.
Are the sounds different?
Now you can make music!